Pullman: Portrait of a Landmark Community

Pullman: Portrait of a Landmark Community

A Photographic Essay by Fred Leavitt
With a View of Historic Pullman by Nancy Miller

The Historic Pullman Foundation
Chicago, 1981

Edited and Designed by Margit Wevang Leavitt

All photographs by Fred Leavitt reprinted with permission
from the Chicago Council on Fine Arts

Acknowledgements

Glenn Anderson, Vivian Anderson, Dennis Banning,
Deborah Bertoletti, Martha and Andrew Brislen,
Robert Bytnar, R.R. Donnelley and Sons Company,
Robert Feie, Alice Grabert, Mary and Ralph Kaye,
Alan Leder, John Lindenbusch, Mrs. Florence Lowden Miller,
Warren Pullman Miller, Liz Olson, Paul Petraitis,
Lyle Schmidt, Guy Scobbie, Mayme Stanley, Carol Tome.

Library of Congress Catalogue Card Number: 81-83923

ISBN: 0-9607136-0-3

Contents

113th and Forrestville, ca. 1890.
This photograph of early Pullman residents is believed to
have been made by James P. Van Vorst, a Pullman
Company photographer for over 40 years.

A Century Recalled, A Heritage Recaptured
by Nancy J. Miller

The photographs in this book capture the heart of an urban neighborhood, one that has been through 100 years of success and strife and still has managed to thrive, due to the determination of its residents. Primarily, the town of Pullman reflects the diverse dreams and goals of strong individuals.

To its founder, George Mortimer Pullman, the attractive, well-run community encouraged hard-working, contented citizen-employees.

To organized labor, Pullman was a test case for union efforts to destroy the "company town" concept that was rapidly gaining favor in the industrial community.

To city planners the world over, Pullman was a vision of the future, the perfectly planned community combining the best of living conditions with the best of economic productivity.

To the people of Pullman, the town of Pullman was their home, a place where they could be born, raise children and grow old. Since January 1, 1881, when the Benson family became the first residents in the town, Pullman has been a place where people could talk over the back fence, hold church dinners, argue politics, plan picnics and parties and dances. For its residents it has long been a source of pride.

Except for its architecture, Pullman is not an unusual community compared to other working-class neighborhoods established during the nation's industrial expansion. As in other urban areas across the country, Italians, Irish, Swedes, Germans and Poles flocked to Pullman for jobs in the shops and found themselves living in the town for the rest of their lives. If many of the children of these settlers moved away when they grew up, many returned to Pullman later on, when it was time to raise their own families.

The present generation is more affluent, better educated and more aware of what Pullman has to offer. One reason they live here today is that they realize that three and four generations of tradition and stability are rare commodities worth preserving in the midst of an increasingly mobile society.

What is unusual and special about Pullman people is their interest in and concern for the community as a whole. Pullman Civic Organization meetings are well attended. Tempers may flare over the merits of one-way streets and four-way stop signs, where children are going to play, how to get potholes repaired and what to do about stray dogs. But the meetings go on, and things get done.

Interest and pride in the community is best illustrated by the Pullman house tour, an annual event that draws tourists and students of history and architecture each autumn to the streets of this 16-square-block area on Chicago's south side.

Home exteriors, many trimmed in the traditional Pullman colors of red and green, are spruced up, and flags wave from front porches. Gardens are personal triumphs. It is not unusual for a stranger to walk down Pullman's tree-shaded streets on a lazy afternoon and be invited into someone's home for a glass of lemonade.

An accurate account of this historic community must begin with a look at the moving force behind the town's development, George Pullman. Historians have tried and failed to define this private and controversial man, but what is important to the people of 20th-century Pullman is how he came to Chicago and why he built his town and factories.

During the early 1850's Pullman's father, a carpenter, contracted with the state of New York to move homes built too close to the soon-to-be-widened Erie Canal. The expe-rience gained from helping his father was to give the younger Pullman the expertise to make his mark in Chicago when he arrived in 1855.

In those early days the growing city of Chicago had a major problem. It was built only a few feet above Lake Michigan, and the streets were often muddy and flooded. The answer was obvious: raise the streets. But what was to be done with the existing buildings? Pullman first gained attention in the city by raising the all-brick Tremont Hotel on Chestnut Street on Chicago's near north side without breaking a window. He was then given a contract to elevate blocks of other buildings downtown. With this work success-fully behind him, his ambition next led him to try building sleeping cars to make rail travel a more comfortable experience.

With a partner he began converting day coaches into sleeping cars but could not com-pete with established producers of custom built sleepers. The Civil War interrupted his car-renovating business, and all available passenger cars were pressed into service for the Union army.

A restless Pullman then went west to the Colorado gold fields where he opened a trad-ing post and operated a sawmill. Profits from the trading post made it possible for him to return to Chicago in the mid-1860's and build the elaborate sleeping car that made railroad history.

"Pioneer," the first true Pullman sleeping car, was a great advancement in comfort and convenience. Taller and wider than other passenger cars, at $25,000 it cost five times more to build than an average sleeper. Pullman gambled that the travelers would welcome the innovations. The railroads, however, were reluctant to spend the time and money to modify bridges and station platforms to accommodate the larger car.

The problem was solved when the Chicago and Alton line made the necessary adjustments to allow the car's momentous debut as part of the funeral train transporting Abraham Lincoln's body from Chicago to Springfield. National attention from the publicity of Lincoln's funeral convinced other railroads to make the changes required to accommodate the luxury car. Over the next 25 years the Pullman Palace Car Company continued to meet the expanding needs of a nation traveling by rail from coast to coast.

Since 1869, Pullman had owned property south of Chicago along Lake Calumet's west bank. In 1880 he decided to buy more land to expand the Pullman Palace Car Company's facilities. More than 4,000 acres were purchased for $800,000, and plans for a model town to be built on the same site as his factory were released to an astonished press.

Pullman told the press that "I have faith in the educational and refining influences of beauty, and beautiful and harmonious surroundings, and hesitate at no expenditure to secure them."

The utilitarian but distinctive architecture and park-like atmosphere provided by Solon S. Beman and Nathan F. Barrett a century ago still reflect this philosophy. These men, under George Pullman's direction, were the first architects in the nation to incorporate an esthetic ideal and community amenities with the most up-to-date building technology.

Across the country tremendous numbers of people concentrated in the cities, attracted by increasing demands for labor. Growing cities were unable to adequately house the thousands of immigrants looking for work. The result was overcrowding, rampant disease and crime. Pullman offered a welcome escape from these intolerable conditions by providing decent housing on spacious streets.

From clay quarried at Lake Calumet that was made into bricks at his plant, Pullman built solid, attractive two- and three-story row houses with plumbing, heat and good ventilation, as well as block houses for single workers. Each building had front and back yards complete with porches, and trees in the parkway.

Elaborate and carefully landscaped parkland, including a lake for swimming and boating, made entering the town by rail an unforgettable experience. An 88-year resident remembered her first glimpse of the town as a 9-year-old child:

"I came to Pullman from Scotland in May, 1891. My father had come here three years before us to work for Pullman. We got off the train at the depot, and there was Lake Vista. There were lovely trees on each side of the street and everybody had grass and lawns. You could see from the train that they had PULLMAN spelled out by Lake Vista, and I knew we were here."

Pullman provided his tenants with everything he thought they could possibly need. Retail stores were housed in the 90-foot-high, 250-foot-long Arcade building until it was torn down in the 1920's. An early version of today's multi-use shopping mall, the Arcade also offered the services of a bank and library, and entertainment through a theater and billiard hall.

Bordering the park were a livery stable, the Greenstone Church and the Hotel Florence. The hotel provided first-class accommodations for visiting dignitaries and craftsmen, but the patronage of residents was discouraged. The hotel did have a bar, but the sale of alcohol was forbidden in the rest of the town as drinking undermined the moral standard set for employees.

Market Hall, a three-story building in the center of town, was the source of fresh meat and produce and served as the social center of Pullman where dances and sporting events were held. Today it is a fire-gutted, one-story building which is being preserved with the hope of it someday being restored for the benefit of the community. Still, older residents remember gathering at the Market Hall to hear the big bands play for summer evening dances and to watch young men compete in boxing and basketball.

An innovation which helped win Pullman the title of the "world's most perfect town" at the Prague International Hygienic and Pharmaceutical Exposition of 1896 was a complex underground sewage system. It collected all runoff and waste and transported it to a model farm three miles away to be used as crop fertilizer.

With nearly 8,000 people living in the town and more moving in every day, an additional Beman-designed neighborhood was built north of the factory. The early years of growth seemed to assure the world that the daring experiment was a success. But there was trouble brewing in the model town. Part of what made Pullman unique was the striving for complete central control, from providing the bricks for the buildings to the books in the library. Unyielding and unbending control of the town helped lead to George Pullman's downfall and the devastating Pullman Strike.

The year 1893 brought a widespread economic depression to the nation. A report that the railroads had a three-year surplus of cars spurred a reorganization of the company. Plants outside of Illinois were closed. Wages were reduced at the Chicago facilities, and in Pullman the work force dropped from 4,500 to 1,100.

An average 28-percent cut showed up in paychecks, but monthly rents in the town remained the same: from $8 for a three-room apartment to $25 for an entire house. Hardest hit were those living in single-family dwellings, where often one-third of the paycheck went for rent.

Pullman had often said that the company was both landlord and employer. He believed that since rents were not raised during prosperous times, they should not be lowered during hard times. However, the reputation the company held for charging exorbitant rents remained, and the monopoly of factory and town became a major issue in the upcoming confrontations.

The spring and summer of 1894 was a period of labor unrest throughout the railroad industry. The American Railway Union, under the leadership of Eugene V. Debs, organized the Pullman Palace Car Company on the loose grounds that because the company operated 20 miles of track all the workers were employed by a railroad. Most of those who joined the union were skilled workers living in the most expensive houses and were, therefore, the hardest hit by the wage cuts.

Early in May, 1894, union negotiators requesting either a wage increase or a rent reduction failed to change George Pullman's firm stand, and on May 10 the workers walked out. The historic strike became the vortex of a storm fed by a national test of wills between American corporations and organized labor.

Charges and countercharges followed the walkout, with each side claiming that the other was responsible for the strike. Unfortunately, while the high-level arguing continued, those who suffered the most were the residents of Pullman.

Many of the wives and children of the strikers also worked for the company in the laundry or the embroidery department. Some quit in sympathy with the union while others were laid off. The result was that entire families were faced with bills to be paid, and they had no income.

Strikers formed a relief committee, and help, in the form of money, food and clothing, came from businesses, unions, charitable organizations and individuals. Local drug stores filled prescriptions at no charge, and medical services were donated. All the aid was not enough, and by the time the strike was a month old, hundreds of families were forced to leave Pullman and find work elsewhere.

As the strike dragged into July, the strain began to affect George Pullman. He became more of a recluse, refusing to grant interviews and spending much of his time in New York. Robert Todd Lincoln, son of the assassinated president, became the spokesman for the company.

In August, with little fanfare, the shops reopened. The majority of former employees turned in their union cards and returned to work. Technically the strike continued, but the flow of supplies and aid to the community was dwindling. The strike ended by default.

Destroyed was the image of the model town solving the capital versus labor conflict. Lost were hundred of thousands of dollars in wages and the reputation of a major national company and its founder. Gained was international notoriety, making "Pullman" synonomous with American labor conflict.

In 1895, Debs was sent to prison, and an Illinois circuit court ruled that the Pullman company could own both town and factory. It was a dubious victory. The next year George

Pullman's health began to fail rapidly, and in 1897, at the age of 66, he died of a heart attack.

One year after his death, the Illinois Supreme Court reversed the lower court's decision, and the Pullman company was ordered to sell all property not used for manufacturing. The town of Pullman was placed on the auction block. By 1909, all property had been sold, and Pullman became a typical industrial community.

Residents were given first option on their homes for 100 times the monthly rent. A current Pullmanite, who was a child during the strike, remembers her parents buying their house in 1907. The rent had been $19.50 a month, so the purchase price was $1,950.

Socially and economically Pullman was no longer a "planned community," but its people were still proud of their town. A Pullman Homeowners' Association was formed in 1908, and one of its first achievements was the construction of a new public school building named for George M. Pullman.

From 1910, through two world wars and a depression, Pullman survived.

Bread went up to 19 cents a loaf, but soup bones were free, and pickles were only a penny apiece. The alleys were paved in the 1920's thanks to a petition passed from neighbor to neighbor. Community pressure also forced the Illinois Central Railroad to raise its track bed on the west side of town to prevent accidents.

During prohibition speakeasys flourished, and whisky flowed in the streets when revenue agents raided. Legal taverns arrived in the 1930's, many opened by old speakeasy operators, and at one time Pullman boasted 15 well patronized bars.

The Hotel Florence, once used for entertaining friends and clients of George Pullman and the Pullman Palace Car Company, became a boardinghouse in 1909. An annex was built in 1915 which then made a total of 120 rooms available for rent, mostly to workers in the Pullman shops, for $3 a week or $30 a month, including three meals a day.

The local version of Rosie the Riveter came to Pullman during World War II, when women took the jobs left by men going to war. Assembly line workers helped build tank parts and artillery shells instead of luxury passenger cars. Pacific-bound Patrol Craft Escorts were launched a few blocks away in Calumet Harbor, including one christened by George Pullman's granddaughter.

Post-war Pullman saw very little change. People continued to live quietly, unaware that their lifestyle was not changing with the times. Suddenly the 1960's arrived, and the town awoke to discover that plans were underway to destroy their home.

In 1960, the City of Chicago published a statement of goals and policies which recommended vast clearance and rebuilding of "blighted and deteriorating areas" in the city. Pullman was designated one of those areas.

As in the past, Pullman residents met the challenge. An emergency meeting was held at the Greenstone Church, and by the time it was called to order concerned citizens filled the building and crowded the sidewalk.

The Pullman Civic Organization, which had been a civil defense group during the war, was revitalized to unify the neighborhood. Homeowners once again began to take pride in the appearance of their homes, to remodel and clean up, to prove to Chicago that Pullman was neither blighted nor deteriorating.

Another crisis came later in the decade when a land developer proposed replacing some of the original Pullman Palace Car Company factory buildings with a budget motel. Now was the time, Pullmanites decided, to preserve their town as an historic site as well as a place to live.

Fast work on the part of a civic committee in 1969 succeeded in getting Pullman designated as the largest National Historic Landmark district in the country. Achieving recognition as a City of Chicago Landmark District proved more difficult. Nevertheless, when 100 percent of resident owners, non-resident owners and mortgage holders voiced their support, the designation was approved.

To obtain funds to buy and protect public buildings, in 1973 the Historic Pullman Foundation was formed. A not-for-profit organization, the foundation first rescued the Historic Pullman Center, once a rooming house and later the Masonic Lodge, for use as a nucleus for community activities.

After the purchase of the Market Hall and the Arcade site, the largest emotional and financial responsibility of the foundation was the "grand old lady," the Hotel Florence, acquired just days before demolition action. The hotel became the foundation's headquarters, and by 1980 most of the exterior and two floors had been restored, and an attractive restaurant/bar was open for business.

Not included in the 1972 city landmark designation, North Pullman has become a focal point of efforts to stabilize the entire Pullman community.

Until recently, absentee landlords and rapid resident turnover in North Pullman discouraged the kind of stability that is found in South Pullman. Working with newly formed civic groups, the foundation is rehabilitating original dwellings in North Pullman, and private developers are converting two abandoned Pullman factory buildings into apartments. The goal of this combined effort is to create a more positive image of North Pullman and to bring life back into an important part of the Pullman Historic District.

The moments of Pullman captured in this book speak for themselves, but the people, those who know Pullman best, the volunteers, the house-tour committee, the young preservationists should have the last word:

"Pullman in 1981 has seen a rebirth of its historic value – it's a sharing of the wisdom and guidance between the older generation and the new residents who have discovered the charm and character that Pullman has to offer .... a sharing of love for the community by all the people who give of their time, energy and talent.

"We are proud of our heritage and of Pullman ... that's why we are here."

In April, 1980, The Chicago Council on Fine Arts in conjunction with the City Architect's Office commissioned Fred Leavitt, a freelance photographer and native Chicagoan, to document the historic community of Pullman in black and white photography for permanent exhibition in a newly constructed municipal building in Pullman. This was the first commission awarded to a photographer under the council's Percent for Art program. As the commission neared completion, the Historic Pullman Foundation concluded that this body of work deserved the attention of a larger audience and undertook its publication in book form to coincide with Pullman's centennial. The foundation observes that the subject of this book is not historic preservation and renovation but is instead the study of a living neighborhood, which happens also to be an historic landmark.

That the community of Pullman has survived strikes, wars, depressions and the very real threat of the wrecker's ball to celebrate its centennial and is, in fact, actively undergoing a rebirth at this time, is due solely to the spirit and dedication of its people, and it is to the people of Pullman that this book is dedicated.

53

60

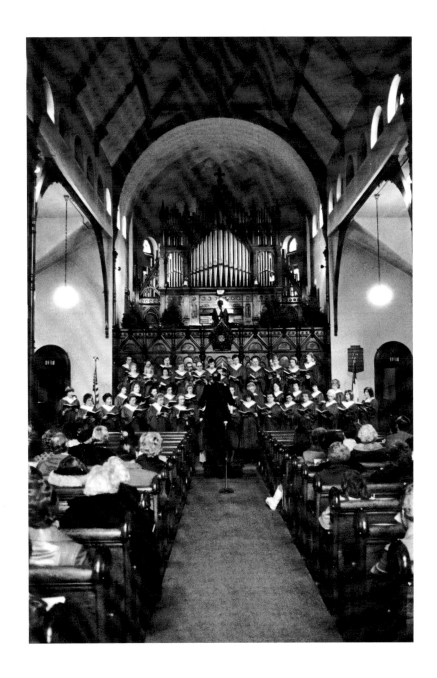